DESIGNER DESSERTS
Coloring Book

Eileen Rudisill Miller

DOVER PUBLICATIONS, INC.
Mineola, New York

NOTE

This scrumptious set of delicious desserts was rendered with the experienced colorist in mind. Select your media, and use the detailed images of cakes, candies, pies, and other tasty treats to experiment with color usage and technique. Plus, the perforated, unbacked pages make displaying your work easy!

Bibliographical Note
Designer Desserts Coloring Book is a new work, first published by Dover Publications, Inc., in 2014.

International Standard Book Number
ISBN-13: 978-0-486-49632-0
ISBN-10: 0-486-49632-5

Manufactured in the United States by Courier Corporation
49632504   2015
www.doverpublications.com